Abraham Lincoln

by Clara Ingram Judson

Illustrated by Polly Jackson

Follett Publishing Company

Chicago

56789

Abraham Lincoln was born on a farm in the state of Kentucky, on February 12, 1809.

When Abraham was two years old, his father took the family to a new farm in Kentucky. They called it Knob Creek Farm.

Abraham's family called him Abe. Abe and his sister, Sarah, helped with the work. They got water from the spring for their mother. They got wood for the fire.

Abe helped with farm work too. Father planted corn. Abe planted pumpkin seeds.

When they were not working, Abe and
Sarah liked to watch the road. They sat
in front of the cabin. People went by
on their way to town.

One day a man on a horse went by. He
had fine clothes and a good horse. Abe
asked his mother who the man was.

"He's a lawyer," Abe's mother said.
"He is going to court in town."

Abe thought the man looked fine.

"I would like to be a lawyer," Abe said.

One day the Lincoln family heard that a new school was opening.

Abe said, "Now I can go and learn to read and write."

In the morning Abe and Sarah washed well. They put on clean clothes. They walked three miles to the little school.

Abe liked school. He learned letters and words. He learned to use numbers.

But soon the teacher went away. There was no more school. Abe was sad.

Abe worked at home, but he wanted to
go to school. He wanted to be a lawyer.

When Abe was seven, his father said
they would leave Knob Creek.

"We're going to Indiana," Father said.

"Where's Indiana?" Sarah wanted to know.

"It's across the Ohio River," said Father.

"Why can't we stay here?" Abe asked.

"We can live better in Indiana," his
father said.

Mother washed clothes. She cooked food to take with them. Soon everything was ready for the Lincoln family to go to Indiana.

The horses carried the clothes and other things. Mother and Father walked. Abe and Sarah walked most of the time too.

After a while they came to the Ohio River. Abe was surprised at how big it was.

They crossed the Ohio River on a big raft. After that they walked for over two days. Then they came to the new farm.

"This is the place," Abe's father said.
"Tomorrow I will start to build a shelter."

"I will get supper now," said Mother.
"But I need water."

"The spring is about a mile away,"
Father said. "Sarah, you go with Abe
and get some water."

Abe and Sarah liked to walk through
the woods. But when they came back, carrying
the water, a mile seemed long.

In the morning, Father began to work.
All the family helped. They built a shelter
with three sides and a roof.

Father said, "That will do for now.
I must cut trees for a corn field."

That winter was very cold. Abe kept
a fire by the open side of the shelter, but
still they were always cold.

Summer came, warm and beautiful. Birds
sang, and flowers were bright in the fields.
Father built a good cabin. Father went
hunting to get food too.

11

The Lincolns had lived in Indiana for two years when Abe's mother died.

Everyone was very sad. Father did not go hunting. Sarah was too young to be a good cook. Abe forgot to get water and to wash. There was no soap, and Sarah did not know how to make more.

After a while Father went back to Kentucky. He left the children to take care of the farm.

Weeks went by. Then one day the children heard a wagon coming. They saw a big wagon with a woman driving. Two girls and a boy sat by her. Father walked beside the wagon.

"I have brought you a new mother," he said.

The new Mrs. Lincoln got down from the wagon. She put her arms around Abe and Sarah.

Mrs. Lincoln cleaned everything. Then she had her things brought in from the wagon.

Abe brought in some books.

"Books!" he said. "You have books!"

"You like to read, Abe?"

"I would like to. But I can't read much. The teacher went away."

"I will help you," his new mother said.

At night Abe read by the light of the fire. His mother helped him with hard words, and he read all her books.

Now and then a teacher came to the school near by. The children went when there was school. But Abe learned more at home.

One day Abe found a dog that was hurt. He took him home and made him well.

"This is my dog," he said to the family.

Abe grew tall and strong. He could
cut logs and make a good fence. He could
plow a field and build a cabin.

He worked for neighbors. Some of them
had a book or two. They let Abe take a
book home to read at night.

Abe always took good care of the books.
But one neighbor's book got wet in the
rain. Abe worked for the neighbor to pay
for it. The man said he could keep the book.
That was the first book Abe owned.

As years passed, Abe worked at many jobs. Sometimes he worked in town.

There were papers to read in town. Abe read about his country and its great men. He read about George Washington. He read about men who made the country's laws.

This made Abe think more about being a lawyer. How could a poor farmer's son begin to study law?

Besides reading, Abe liked working by the river. He was glad when a man asked him to help build a boat. When it was built, they loaded it with corn and ham and bacon.

"I want you to go with me, Abe," the man said. "We start for New Orleans tomorrow."

They went down the Ohio River and down the Mississippi River to New Orleans. There they sold the corn and ham and bacon. They sold the logs that made the boat too!

In New Orleans, Abe walked about, looking at everything. He saw many things he liked.

But he saw one thing he did not like. He saw people who were slaves. He was glad to go back to Indiana, where there were no slaves.

When Abe got home, his father said:

"We're going to Illinois. I can get good land there with water near."

Abe helped put their things in the big wagon, and the Lincolns went to Illinois.

The weather was cold. There was ice on the rivers. After crossing one little river, Abe heard a bark. His dog was still on the other side.

His father and the others went on. But Abe walked back through the cold water. He took his dog and carried him across the river.

At the new farm, Abe helped build a cabin. He made fences and plowed fields.

Then one day Abe said good-by to his family. He was twenty-one years old. He was a man now. He was going away to learn to be a lawyer.

Abe traveled about doing many kinds of work. Sometimes he got little jobs to pay for food and a place to sleep. After a while he came to a place called New Salem.

New Salem people liked Abe. He liked them. Some had books that they let Abe read. One man was a teacher. He helped Abe to read better.

One day Abe found an old law book. It was hard reading, but he read it all. After that he wanted more law books. He got a job as postmaster. He often read his law books as he traveled around with letters for farmers.

New Salem people knew Abe was fair and honest and a hard worker. They knew he was studying law. They elected him to help make laws for the state of Illinois.

Abe did good work as a law maker. He
kept on studying. When he was twenty-eight
years old, he was ready to be a lawyer.

Abe opened an office in Springfield,
Illinois. Friends came to ask his help.
People who did not know him came for help too.

The old friends still called him "Abe."
But the other people called him "Mr. Lincoln."

People always liked to hear Abe talk.
He had a way of saying things that made them
think. Sometimes he made them laugh too.

One day a man asked him, "Mr. Lincoln,
how long do you think a man's legs should be?"

Abe looked at the man's short legs and
at his own long ones. "Well," he said, "I think
they should be long enough to reach the floor."

After he opened his law office, Abraham
Lincoln married a pretty girl from Kentucky.
They had four sons.

Mr. Lincoln worked hard. But he played
with his boys too. They liked to play ball.

Years passed. Mr. Lincoln made more friends. People liked him and believed in him. They elected him to go to Washington to make laws for the country.

At this time most people in the South were farmers. Some people had very large farms. Many people in the South had slaves to work the farms and grow cotton and other things. They wanted to keep the slaves.

In the North, farms were not so large. Many people worked in factories. They did not want slaves. They did not need them. Many people believed it was wrong to have other people as slaves.

People in the North and the South argued about the slaves.

They argued about government too. Men at Washington worked to make laws that would be fair to the North and the South. But they could not.

Some people said that the North should
be one country and the South should be another
country. Then each could make its own laws.

Abraham Lincoln said no. He thought
the United States must stay all one country.

He went to different parts of the country
and made speeches. Mr. Lincoln said, "We are
one country, the United States of America.
We must stay united."

Many people liked what Lincoln said.

They asked him to run for president.

There were many parades and speeches.
Then the day came when the people voted.
Abraham Lincoln was elected president.

He said good-by to friends in Springfield.

"Let us hope that all will be well,"
he said. "God be with you and with me."

Then Abraham Lincoln went to Washington.

States in the South had said they would
leave the United States if Lincoln was
elected president. They did leave. Soon
the War Between the States began.

It was a very dreadful war, because it was between people who had been friends. It was often brother against brother and father against son.

Each side believed it was fighting for what was right. The War Between the States lasted four long hard years. The South was hurt most, for much of the war was fought there.

When it was over, the slaves were free. The states were still united.

Now that the war was over, President
Lincoln wanted to help the South to become
strong again. He had good plans for the
country he loved.

But before he could try any of his
plans, a man killed him.

People all over the country were very,
very sad. "What shall we do?" they asked.
"We needed Abraham Lincoln."

But Abraham Lincoln was dead.

After he was dead, people remembered the good things Abraham Lincoln did and said. They remembered how wise he was and how fair and honest. They named towns and schools, parks and streets, in his honor.

Today everyone remembers his birthday, February 12. People all over the world know Abraham Lincoln as a great man, one of the greatest Americans. He loved his country and was a friend of all the people. He wanted his country to stay always united and always free.

ABRAHAM LINCOLN

Reading Level: Level Three. *Abraham Lincoln* has a total vocabulary of 362 words. It has been tested in third grade classes, where it was read with ease.

Uses of This Book: An excellent introduction to history. This interesting biography will help primary children to understand why Abraham Lincoln was one of the greatest Americans. Good for older slow readers.

Word List

5 Abraham	and	went	can	leave(s)
Lincoln(s)	sister	by	learn(ed)	we('re)
was	Sarah	way	read(ing)	Indiana
born	help(ed)	town	write	where('s)
on	with	one(s)	morning	know
a	work(ing)(ed)(er)	day(s)	wash(ed)	across
farm(s)	got	man('s)	well	Ohio
in	water	horse(s)	put	river(s)
the	from	he('s)	clean(ed)	why
state(s)	spring	fine	walk(ed)(ing)	can't
of	for	clothes	three	stay
Kentucky	their	good	mile(s)	here
February	mother	ask(ed)	little	live(d)
when	wood(s)	who	letters	better
two	fire	lawyer	words **9**	she
years	too	said	use	cook(ed)
old	planted	is	numbers	food
his	corn	go(ing)	but	take
father	pumpkin	court	soon	them
took	seeds	thought	teacher	everything
family **6**	were	look(ed)(ing)	away	ready
to	not	I	there	carried
new	like(d)	would	no	other(s)
they	watch	be(ing)	more	thing(s)
called	road **7**	heard	sad	most
it(s)('s)	sat	that **8**	at	time
Knob Creek	front	school	home	after
him	cabin	open(ing)(ed)	want(ed)	while
Abe('s)	people	now	seven	came